KINGFISHER
READERS

level
3

Astronauts

Hannah Wilson

KINGFISHER

KINGFISHER

First published 2015 by Kingfisher
an imprint of Macmillan Children's Books
a division of Macmillan Publishers Limited
20 New Wharf Road, London N1 9RR
Basingstoke and Oxford
Associated companies throughout the world
www.panmacmillan.com

Series editor: Polly Goodman
Literacy consultant: Hilary Horton

ISBN 978-07534-3795-7
Copyright © Macmillan Publishers Ltd 2015

9 8 7 6 5 4 3 2 1

1TR/1014/WKT/UG/105MA

A CIP catalogue record for this book is available from the British Library.

Printed in China

Picture credits
The Publisher would like to thank the following for permission to reproduce their material.
Every care has been taken to trace copyright holders. However, if there have been unintentional
omissions or failure to trace copyright holders, we apologize and will, if informed, endeavour
to make corrections in any future edition.
Top = t; Bottom = b; Centre = c; Left = l; Right = r
Cover NASA; Pages 4, 5, 6 NASA; 7t, 7b RIA Novosti/Science Photo Library; 8, 9l, 9r NASA; 10 Mark
Paternostro/Science Photo Library; 11l NASA/Science Photo Library; 11r NASA; 12 NASA/Science
Photo Library; 13 RIA Novosti/Science Photo Library; 14 Starsem/Francis Demange/Science Photo Library;
15 NASA/Bill Ingalls; 16 European Space Agency, T. Peake/Science Photo Library; 17, 18t, 18b, 19, 20,
21t, 21b NASA; 22–23 NASA/Science Photo Library; 24–25 NASA; 24b, 25b NASA/Bill Ingalls; 26 NASA/
Science Photo Library; 27 Mark Greenberg/Virgin Galactic/Getty Images; 28 Carol & Mike Werner/Science
Photo Library.

Contents

What are astronauts?   4

Early astronauts   6

Moonwalk   8

Emergency in space!   10

Astronaut training   12

On the ground   14

Three, two, one, lift off!   16

Life on a space station   18

All in a day's work   20

Spacewalk   22

Returning to Earth   24

Tourists in space   26

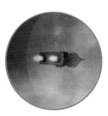

The future of space travel   28

Glossary   30

Index   32

What are astronauts?

Astronauts are space explorers, highly trained pilots or scientists who travel into space. Space begins about 100 kilometres above the Earth.

Did you know?
The word 'astronaut' means 'star sailor'.

Astronauts need to wear special spacesuits to survive in space. The suits protect them from the burning hot and freezing cold temperatures, and give them oxygen to breathe.

Let's find out how astronauts train for their **space missions** and how huge rockets blast them into space. Let's find out how they travel to the Moon and what life is like on a **space station**!

Early astronauts

The first creatures to reach space were fruit flies. They were launched into space in a rocket, in 1947.

In 1961, a chimpanzee called Ham spent almost 17 minutes in space before his **space capsule** splashed safely back into the Earth's ocean.

Ham the Astrochimp
Ham was trained to push levers inside the space capsule.

The first person to travel into space was the **cosmonaut** Yuri Gagarin, also in 1961. Gagarin was strapped inside a space capsule at the top of a rocket.

Yuri Gagarin inside
the capsule ——————

About ten minutes
after the launch, the
rocket dropped away
leaving the capsule
in space!

Moonwalk

American astronaut Neil Armstrong was the first person to walk on the Moon. In 1969, a huge rocket blasted Armstrong, Michael Collins and Edwin Aldrin into space. It took three days for their spacecraft to reach the Moon.

Moon landing
Armstrong and Aldrin travelled down to the surface of the Moon in a small landing craft, called *Eagle*.

The astronauts had fun moonwalking! Their strides were huge and bouncing because of the weak **gravity** on the Moon. Their footprints will remain there for millions of years because there is no weather to destroy them.

footprint

Famous words
Armstrong stepped on to the Moon, and said, "That's one small step for man, one giant leap for mankind."

Emergency in space!

In 1970, Commander Jim Lovell and two other astronauts were on their way to the Moon when they heard a loud bang. An oxygen tank had exploded! Astronauts need oxygen to breathe, but also to make water and electricity on the spacecraft.

Famous words
When he heard the explosion, Jim Lovell told the control centre in Houston, USA, "Houston, we've had a problem."

explosion

To save electricity for the journey back to Earth, the astronauts turned off some equipment. After almost four exhausting and frightening days, the astronauts' space capsule splashed down into the Pacific Ocean. They were safe at last.

A crane lifts the capsule out of the ocean.

The astronauts arrive home.

Astronaut training

All astronauts have to learn how spacecraft and space stations work. They must know every button, dial and switch, and how to make repairs. Astronauts also practise experiments to perform in space.

Vomit comets

Special aircraft let astronauts feel what **weightlessness** is like in space. They are called 'vomit comets' as people often feel sick inside them!

Astronauts exercise to become fit and strong. They practise **spacewalking** by **scuba diving** in a swimming pool containing a model space station. This prepares them for spacewalking outside the real station.

On the ground

Keeping clean
Engineers wear special clothes and hairnets to stop germs and dirt damaging the spacecraft.

Fewer than ten astronauts travel into space each year, but thousands of people work hard to get them there and back safely. Engineers design, build and test spacecraft and new sections for space stations. Doctors work out what food, medicine and exercise the astronauts will need.

A control centre, like the one in Houston, closely monitors the spacecraft or space station during a mission. This centre is called **mission control**. Controllers use computers to track the location of the spacecraft and check that its equipment is working properly. They also talk to the astronauts in space.

Three, two, one, lift off!

It's launch day! After breakfast, the astronauts put on their launch suits. They travel up to the cockpit of the spacecraft in a lift.

Launch suits

Astronauts wear special suits during launch and landing. The suits protect them if there is a problem with the oxygen or **air pressure** inside the spacecraft.

The countdown begins. Then, "…three, two, one, lift off!" The rocket rises slowly and smoothly from the launch pad.

The astronauts are pressed into their seats as the rocket speeds up. The four boosters and then the central rocket drop away. After nine minutes, the engines switch off and the astronauts float about weightless. They are in space!

cockpit

central rocket

booster rocket

Life on a space station

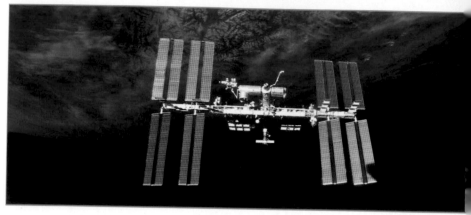

The International Space Station (ISS) is a large spacecraft and science laboratory that **orbits** the Earth. There are usually six astronauts living on the ISS.

Bedtime
Astronauts zip themselves into sleeping bags fastened to walls.

Mealtimes can be tricky because the food floats around! Astronauts eat some food from pouches using a spoon. Water is also stored in pouches. Astronauts suck it out to drink and squirt it on to cloths for washing.

All in a day's work

On board the International Space Station, astronauts work hard as scientists. They study how plants grow in space and they make medicines.

Sometimes the astronauts perform experiments on themselves. They test their own eyesight or take some blood, to help doctors understand how space travel affects the human body.

When astronauts aren't working, they relax by reading books, watching films or even playing the guitar.

space station

spacecraft

Travelling to the ISS
Astronauts travel to the ISS in a spacecraft, which attaches to the space station.

Spacewalk

If something needs repairing on the outside of the space station, it is time for a spacewalk! The astronaut puts on a special spacesuit. The suit provides heating and cooling systems, oxygen for breathing and a computer to monitor the equipment.

Astronauts leave the space station through two doors. They must lock the first door tightly behind them before opening the second door, so no air escapes from the station.

Tethered
A tether (rope) stops the astronaut floating away. If the tether breaks, the astronaut can use a **jet pack** to fly back to the station.

Returning to Earth

Astronauts travel from the space station back to Earth in a small space capsule. It takes about three hours to reach the Earth's **atmosphere**. The capsule has a special heat shield to prevent it from burning up as it enters the atmosphere.

Three astronauts are still inside this capsule, which has just landed.

A space capsule enters the atmosphere.

Once safely inside the atmosphere, parachutes slow down the capsule before it lands on the ground. Many space missions have ended with spacecraft landing in the sea.

Back on Earth
After returning from space, astronauts rest and have medical checks.

Tourists in space

Astronauts are highly trained professionals who dedicate their lives to space science and exploration. But what if someone like you or me wanted to travel into space? You can be a space tourist, as long as you have plenty of money to pay for the trip!

First space tourist
In 2001, Dennis Tito paid about US$20 million to spend almost six days on the ISS.

Engineers are racing to design new spacecraft for tourists. Tourist spacecraft will not orbit the Earth like the International Space Station. They will travel only just beyond the Earth's atmosphere. Here, passengers will experience a few minutes of weightlessness and be able to see the curve of the Earth's surface.

This spacecraft can carry six passengers.

The future of space travel

It is difficult for humans to explore space because it takes so long to travel the huge distances. The *Voyager 1* **probe** took 35 years to travel outside our **Solar System**!

It would take thousands of years to reach another solar system, so we need faster spacecraft. One day, it might be possible for astronauts to survive very long journeys by being put into a deep sleep!

ASTRONAUT TIMELINE

1961 Yuri Gagarin is the first man in space.

1963 Valentina Tereshkova is the first woman in space.

1969 Neil Armstrong is the first person to walk on the Moon.

1981 John Young is the first commander of NASA's space shuttle.

2000 William Shepherd commands the ISS's first crew.

ASTRONAUT RECORDS

Most time spent in space: 803 days (Sergei Krikalev, 1998–2005)

Longest single spaceflight by a woman: 195 days (Sunita Williams, 2007)

Longest spacewalk: 8 hours 56 mins (Susan Helms and James Voss, 2001)

Youngest astronaut in space: 25 years old (Gherman Titov, 1961)

Oldest astronaut in space: 77 years old (John Glenn, 1998)

Glossary

air pressure The pressing action of air.

atmosphere The layer of gases that surround a planet.

cosmonaut The Russian word for astronaut.

gravity The force that pulls objects towards each other.

jet pack A small backpack that blasts out gas to move an astronaut during a spacewalk.

mission control The room or building from which a space mission is controlled.

orbit To travel around an object in space.

probe A small spacecraft that is controlled by computers rather than a pilot.

scuba diving Swimming underwater with a tank of air for breathing.

Solar System The collection of planets, moons and rocks that orbit the Sun.

space capsule A small section of a spacecraft in which an astronaut sits.

space mission A trip into space by astronauts or probes to learn more about Earth and the Solar System.

space station A large spacecraft and science laboratory that orbits the Earth. The International Space Station has orbited the Earth since 1998.

spacewalking Going outside a space station or spacecraft to carry out a repair or an experiment.

weightlessness The floating sensation that astronauts experience in space.

Index

Aldrin, Edwin 8
Armstrong, Neil
  8, 9, 29
atmosphere 24, 27

Collins, Michael 8
control centres 10,
  15

engineers 14, 27

food 14, 19

Gagarin, Yuri 6,
  7, 29
gravity 9

launch 5, 6, 7,
  16–17
Lovell, Jim 10, 29

medicines 14, 20
Moon 5, 8–9, 10

moonwalking 8, 9

probes 28

rockets 5, 6, 7, 17

scuba diving 13
sleeping 18
Solar System 28
space capsules 6,
  7, 11, 24, 25
space stations 12,
  13, 14, 15, 18–21,
  22, 23, 24, 26, 27
spacesuits 4, 5, 16,
  22
spacewalking 13,
  22–23

Tito, Dennis 26

weightlessness 12,
  27